Abigail's Orchard

BY ELAINE WILLIAMS

**Abigail's Orchard
and
Fun With Words**
By Elaine Williams

Copyright © 2015

All rights reserved.

Scripture taken from
New King James Version

Library of Congress Number: 2015937322
International Standard Book Number: 978-1-60126-451-0

Printed 2015 by
Masthof Press
*219 Mill Road
Morgantown, PA 19543-9516*

Dedicated to
SARA GRACE JONES

TABLE OF CONTENTS

Orchards 1
    The Good-Fruit Tree 3
    The Best Fruit of All – Love 4
    The Praise Fruit – Joy 5
    The Fearless Fruit – Peace 6
    The Patient Fruit – Long-suffering 7
    The Tender Fruit – Kindness 8
    The Gracious Fruit – Goodness 9
    The Dependable Fruit – Faithfulness 10
    The Humble Fruit – Gentleness 11
    The Powerful Fruit – Self Control 12
Abigail's Orchard 13
    Diamante Poetry 17
Grandparents and Great-Grandparents 18
David's Family 20
David's Great-Grandmother Ruth 22
Ruth's Fruit 24
    Two Diamantes About Ruth and Boaz 26
King David's Great- Great- Great- . . .
    Granddaughter 27
Abigail's Orchard Puzzle 29

ORCHARDS

An orchard is a fruit farm. If you ever visited an orchard in the late summer or early fall when the fruit is ripe, you probably saw rows and rows of apple, peach, and cherry trees along with hundreds of pumpkins in the patch. On a warm, sunny day, you can even smell the fruit before it is picked. Schoolchildren often take field trips to the orchard.

Many orchards allow people to come and pick fruit. Have you ever picked strawberries? They are one of the earliest fruits to ripen in the spring. They grow on small plants, so you have to bend down and move the leaves around to find the juicy red berries. Pap (my dad) picked strawberries when he was a boy about 80 years ago. He got paid a penny for each quart of berries he picked. One day he made $3.84. Years later, his granddaughter picked berries. Although she picked less berries, she made more money than Pap, but she did not enjoy that job.

Orchards have many kinds of fruit trees. In our part of the country these include apple, peach, pear, plum, and cherry. Oranges, grapefruit, apricot, lime, kiwi, mango, and others grow in warm climates such as Florida and California. Bananas, figs, pomegranates, and coconuts grow on trees, too—mostly in warmer countries.

In addition, orchards often have blueberry, raspberry, and blackberry bushes. Usually there is a patch of pumpkins somewhere in the orchard. There might be grapevines; however, there are special gardens called vineyards for growing grapes. Some orchards also include nut trees—such as walnuts, pecans, and almonds (but not peanuts—they grow under the ground).

Much hard work goes into taking care of an orchard, such as trimming the branches, fertilizing, protecting the fruit from bugs, and moving the strawberry plants most years; but all the hard work is worth it when it's time to harvest the fruit and enjoy it—fresh from the plant, in a pie or cobbler, in jelly, or as juice.

God created fruit trees on the 3rd day of Creation. Grapes, figs, and pomegranates are some of the fruits mentioned in the Bible. A sad thing about fruit in the Bible is right at the beginning. Adam and Eve were allowed to eat from every fruit tree in the Garden of Eden except for one very special tree. As you may know, they disobeyed the only rule that God gave them— they ate fruit from the Tree of Knowledge of Good and Evil (Genesis 3). Because of that, all of us are born with sinful hearts (Romans 5:12).

Imagine that—because they disobeyed one rule just one time—they had to leave the Garden, and life changed for the rest of us who have been born since then. Our sinfulness separates us from God. Thankfully, He made a way to undo the punishment for us—Jesus took our punishment when He died on the cross. Then on Easter He arose, and now He is in heaven preparing a place for us.

THE GOOD-FRUIT TREE

What is your favorite fruit—strawberries, blueberries, bananas, grapes, apples, peaches, oranges, or maybe pineapple? Most boys and girls (and adults) prefer fruit over vegetables. Fruit is sweet and can be eaten with your fingers—most of the time. It is so good that it can be a special treat like a dessert all by itself sometimes.

Another way we use the word "fruit" is to describe the result of our words or actions. For example, this book is the fruit of my work. The fruit of a carpenter's work could be a table. The fruit of labor in the kitchen might be a special meal or treat. Perhaps the fruit of an art project is an award or medal. The fruit of studying your spelling words should be a good grade on the test. Good actions produce good fruit.

On the other hand, the fruit of disobedience might be a time out (or even something worse). The fruit of stealing could mean a person gets arrested by the police. The fruit of eating the wrong things may result in very poor health. Bad decisions produce bad fruit.

The Bible says people are like fruit trees. Jesus warned the people to be careful about false prophets—those who preach things that are not true. He said, "You will know them by their fruits. . . . Every good tree bears good fruit, but a bad tree bears bad fruit" (Matthew 7:15-20). When we ask Jesus to be our Savior, we become a good-fruit tree. We are to be fruitful in every good work and also full of good fruits. Make sure that people looking at your "fruit" will know that it came from a good tree.

THE BEST FRUIT OF ALL — LOVE

If you were a fruit, which one would you like to be? Strawberries are so pretty nestled among the green leaves. But if there is too much rain, they get rotten very quickly. Blueberries are good, but they must be protected or the birds will swoop in and eat them off the bush. Apples are delicious—so much that the deer like to eat them off the trees at night. Fresh fruit right off the tree or vine or bush is the very best! Pineapple out of a can is good, but fresh pineapple is so much better!

When we get saved by accepting God's gift of eternal life, we have God's Spirit with us all the time. He will help us to produce good fruit. The Bible lists 9 fruits that should be growing on our good-fruit tree. They are called the Fruit of the Spirit (Galatians 5:22-23).

Love is at the top of the list. If we have true love for God and other people, the other 8 fruits will be there automatically. God's greatest commandment is for us to love Him and to love one another. When we have this kind of love, we are willing to give up what we want so that someone else can have what they want or need. We show people that we love them by doing good things (helping with the chores) or spending time with them, saying nice words, or giving them a gift or a smile or a hug. God loved us so much that He *gave* His Son.

Loving God and others means that we do not envy other people, we are not proud or rude or selfish or happy about bad things. When we love, we are patient, happy about the truth, hopeful, and kind (1 Corinthians 13).

THE PRAISE FRUIT — JOY

What is your favorite Sunday school or church song? During quiet times do you ever realize the words and tune of that song are in your mind? Perhaps you hum or actually sing that song during the day—or even whistle it. Do you know the song, "I Have the Joy, Joy, Joy, Joy Down in My Heart. WHERE?" It's a fun song to sing, and joy is the next thing that should be growing on our good-fruit tree.

Many people think they have joy when they are happy. But when something happens that makes them unhappy, they think they can't have joy. That's just not true. Joy is more than happiness. Joy is when we are satisfied because we know God loves us no matter what is happening in our lives. We are commanded to rejoice in the Lord always (Philippians 4:4). The fruit of our lips is giving thanks and praise to God (Hebrews 13:15).

Do you remember when Paul and Silas were thrown into jail—not for doing something bad, but because they were telling people about Jesus? You would think they would be sad and have a pouty lip. But they didn't. What were they doing in jail at midnight? Singing! Then God sent an earthquake that opened the prison doors and loosened their chains. The jail keeper and his family got saved that night.

So just remember, even when things aren't going the way you want them to go, be joyful and watch God work things out. Let people see your good fruit.

THE FEARLESS FRUIT — PEACE

Are there things that frighten you or cause you to worry? You don't have to be afraid of monsters in the closet or under the bed, because there are no monsters there. People are afraid and worried about many things—their health, friendships, the weather, not enough money, and the condition of the world. But worrying doesn't change things.

God doesn't want us to worry. He knows everything and has the power to take care of it all. Jesus told the disciples He would give them His peace and they should not be afraid (John 14:27). Our job is to trust Him—especially when things seem to be out of control. This is not easy, but there are two things you can do that will help you to have peace.

#1 – Pray. We can pray to God anytime and anywhere about anything. The Bible says we are not to worry about anything, but to thankfully ask God for what we need, and His peace will be with us (Philippians 4:6-7). Tell God about your problems—with friends, schoolwork, or things that make you sad and fearful. And then trust Him.

#2 – Know and think about God's Word. God promises to keep us peaceful when we think about Him and Bible verses that we've learned (Isaiah 26:3).

When we have peace, we also have joy and can sing because of the love of God in our hearts.

THE PATIENT FRUIT — LONG-SUFFERING

Some fruits ripen quickly—like strawberries; others, like pumpkins and watermelons, need a longer growing season. It's hard to wait for fruit to ripen. Young children want to pick the fruit before it is ready (and sometimes they *do* pick it too soon). God made so many different kinds of fruit for us to enjoy.

The next Fruit of the Spirit is one that seems to take a long time to develop. It is called long-suffering or patience. I don't know anyone who likes to suffer or wait for things to get better. We want things our way—right now! There are many verses in the Bible that tell us God is long-suffering toward us when we are not being the good-fruit trees that He wants us to be. Since we were created in the image of God, we are supposed to be long-suffering toward those who bother us. That means we are to hang in there and not strike back when people say things about us or do things to us that make us mad.

There will be times when we need to forgive people for things they say and do. Forgiveness is a hard thing—easy to say, but hard to do.

Joseph, the fellow in the Old Testament who had 10 older mean brothers, is a great example of this fruit. His brothers sold him. He suffered many things, but years later he had the opportunity to forgive them and to show kindness to them.

Hang in there as your fruit ripens. Show love, joy, and peace as you watch how God will work things out for your good.

THE TENDER FRUIT — KINDNESS

What does your mom say when you are around a baby? Probably she says, "Be careful" or "Be gentle." She doesn't want the baby to get hurt. She would say the same thing if you were with someone who just had surgery. It's easy to be gentle and kind to those we love and people who need our help. But according to the Bible, we are to be gentle and kind to *everyone*! You've probably learned the verse Ephesians 4:32. Say it with me. "Be kind to one another, tenderhearted, forgiving one another." Notice the special words: *kind* and *tender*. They go together. We need to be kind in the way we treat others and how we talk to them and about them.

This might be even more difficult than being long-suffering and patient, because with kindness we are to be courteous and polite *especially to those who do not deserve it.* This is called mercy. God shows much mercy to us; and, because we are made in His image, we are to show mercy to others.

King Saul was very jealous of David and tried to kill him several times. David went into hiding to protect himself. King Saul and his soldiers went looking for David. One time when the king was resting in a cave, David sneaked in and could have killed him, but he didn't. That's a good example of mercy (1 Samuel 24). Can you think of other people who were tender and kind?

I hope your good-fruit tree is getting full of love, joy, peace, and long-suffering as you show kindness to others.

THE GRACIOUS FRUIT — GOODNESS

Don't you just love getting gifts? I do, especially when it's not even my birthday or Christmas. It shows me that someone cares about me—loves me! Getting something good when we deserve a punishment is called grace.

It's nice to get these gracious gifts, but the Fruit of the Spirit means that we are the ones who should be *giving* these gifts to others. They don't have to be special things; it's even better to do good things for people. God actually created us to do good works (Ephesians 2:10). Colossians 1:10 reminds us to be "fruitful in every good work." Remember, this isn't doing good things just for people we like. Jesus told His disciples, "Love your enemies, bless those who curse you, do good to those who hate you, and pray for those who spitefully use you" (Matthew 5:44). But 1 Corinthians 13:3 warns us that if we do lots of good works without love—it doesn't count for anything.

I'm beginning to think that each fruit takes a little longer to ripen than the ones that came before it. What do you think? Be good to your friends, but be extra nice to those who are not nice to you. That's gracious living.

THE DEPENDABLE FRUIT — FAITHFULNESS

Are you responsible to do some chores around your home—like setting or clearing the table, making your bed, taking out the trash, sweeping the kitchen floor, or folding laundry? I wonder if you automatically do it when you are supposed to or if your mom or dad reminds you every day to do what you are responsible for. Hopefully, you are dependable and do it on your own. That shows you are growing up and maturing.

Faithfulness is the character of doing what you are supposed to do, when you are supposed to do it, and in the way it is to be done. God wants us to be faithful in everything we do, but especially in our relationship with Him. We should read our Bible and pray every day. We should tell other people about God and what He has done for us. He commands us to be faithful (1 Corinthians 4:2).

A special man and a special lady in the Bible are excellent examples of faithful, dependable good-fruit trees. You may think of others.

Daniel was a man of prayer. The people he worked with knew that he prayed at least 3 times every day. Even when they made a bad law that said people could not pray to anyone but the king, Daniel remained faithful to God. That's why he landed in the lion's den, but God kept him safe and proved to the king that God was powerful.

You can read about Anna serving at the temple for many years. She got to see Baby Jesus because she was faithful (Luke 2:36-37).

Remember to do your chores with a joyful spirit—no complaining allowed!

THE HUMBLE FRUIT — GENTLENESS

Do you know people who are proud and loud? They try to make others think they are the best at whatever they are doing at the moment. They think they are too good to be around the rest of us. No one really enjoys being around them! Satan used to be one of God's beautiful angels, but he became proud and wanted to be in God's place. That's when he lost his place in heaven.

God does not want us to be proud. The opposite is "gentle, humble, or meek." Humble people are gentle and kind. They do not draw attention to themselves. They do what they are supposed to do—love, be joyful and peaceful, do kind things for others faithfully—without bragging about it or drawing attention to themselves.

If you remember what true love is, you will understand that gentleness or meekness means that we are to do and give to others rather than be concerned with what we want for ourselves. We respect others' wishes and needs above our own.

Although Moses was a great leader of the Israelites, he was not a proud man. He didn't think he was capable of doing the job, but God assured him that He would help him. When the Israelites sinned, Moses asked God to forgive them; otherwise, he would be willing to take their punishment (Exodus 32:32). Wow! Jesus was meek when He came to earth as a baby, grew up, and died on the cross in our place.

Keep a close watch on this fruit. It seems to disappear quickly.

THE POWERFUL FRUIT — SELF CONTROL

Are you strong? Do you have a lot of power when you run? Meat, vegetables, and milk will help to make your body stronger and more powerful. Fresh air and exercise are good for us, too.

The last Fruit of the Spirit will show how strong your spirit and heart are. Self control is the fruit of being able to say "no" to things that are not good for you or to things that you should not do. It might be deciding not to get angry when someone does or says something to you or about you. Perhaps you decide not to spend time watching TV when you should be doing something better. Maybe you determine that you will not say words that are mean or bad. Self control is also saying "yes" to the things we should do, like eating the right foods, spending and saving money wisely, and obeying God's Word.

This fruit, as well as the others, is difficult to grow. It takes a lot of determination and prayer that God will help you. When you have self control, you won't strike back, but you'll be long-suffering. You won't look the other way when you see someone who needs your help. You will be faithful in your responsibilities.

Joseph and Daniel are excellent examples of self control. A special lady in the Bible had a whole orchard of good-fruit trees in her life. I'll tell you about her on the next page.

ABIGAIL'S ORCHARD

Abigail was a beautiful lady who lived long ago. Her name means "cause or source of joy"—maybe because her parents were so happy when she was born. We learn about her in the Bible. In those days and in that country, many women did not have a choice about whom they would marry. Often the parents arranged the marriage between the bride and groom. The bride's parents wanted their daughter to marry a rich man. This may be what happened to Abigail, because she was married to a rich man. (In those days, people did not keep track of how much money they had in the bank. They counted their herds of cattle, donkeys, sheep, and goats.) Abigail's husband, Nabal, was a sheep master who had 3,000 sheep and 1,000 goats and shepherds who took care of his animals. However, Nabal was a very mean, hateful man.

Before David became king over Israel, he and his soldiers provided protection for animals and their keepers out in the fields, including Nabal's shepherds and sheep. When it was time to shear the sheep (cut off their wool), Nabal and his shepherds were busy in the fields for many days. Then they had a great feast.

David sent 10 young men to go and ask Nabal for some food as a payment for their protection. Most sheep masters were happy to share their food with those who gave protection to their animals and workers. But Nabal would not give any food to David and his men. The men came back and reported to David everything that Nabal said. This made David so angry that he planned an attack against Nabal and his men. He told 400 of his men to get their swords and prepare to do battle.

One of Nabal's servants went immediately and told Nabal's wife Abigail everything that happened. She quickly gathered a lot of food and loaded it onto donkeys—200 loaves of bread, raisins, figs, meat, and drink. She sent her servants ahead, and then she got on a donkey and started down the hill to meet David and his 400 soldiers.

As Abigail came down the side of a hill, David and his men were coming toward her. When she got to where David could see her, she got off her donkey and bowed down to him as to a king. She was willing to take the blame for what Nabal did. She asked David to take the food as payment for all the work that they did and reminded him that when he would become king, he would not want this battle to be a part of his past.

David and his men took the food and promised her that no harm would come to Nabal or his men. Abigail returned to her home. The next morning she told Nabal about the danger he had put them in by refusing to give David some food. Nabal became ill and died about 10 days later.

When David heard about Nabal's death, he asked Abigail to marry him. Eventually David became King, and Abigail lived in the palace! (1 Samuel 25:2-42)

The Bible doesn't tell us what all Nabal and Abigail had besides the sheep and goats, but they probably had some fruit trees on their property. She certainly took a lot of figs and raisins to David. But we do know that Abigail was a good-fruit tree because of the way she lived. Think about the Fruits of the Spirit and how Abigail demonstrated them in her life.

LOVE – She loved her mean, hateful husband enough to risk her own life to save his.
"By this we know love, because He (Jesus) laid down His life for us. And we also ought to lay down our lives for the brethren." -1 John 3:16

JOY – Her name means "Source or cause of Joy."
"Do not sorrow, for the joy of the Lord is your strength."
- Nehemiah 8:10

PEACE – She made peace with David by her quick actions and kind words.
"If it is possible, as much as depends on you, live peaceably with all men." - Romans 12:18

LONG-SUFFERING – She patiently suffered much as Nabal's wife.

"When you do good and suffer, if you take it patiently, this is commendable before God." - 1 Peter 2:20

KINDNESS – She was polite and courteous.
"What is desired in a man is kindness."
- Proverbs 19:22

GOODNESS – She generously gave food to David.
"Love your enemies, do good to those who hate you, bless those who curse you, and pray for those who spitefully use you." - Luke 6:27-28

FAITHFULNESS – She remained with Nabal despite his meanness.
"It is required in stewards that one be found faithful."
- 1 Corinthians 4:2

GENTLENESS – She humbled herself and bowed herself down before David.
"Put on tender mercies, kindness, humility, meekness, long-suffering, bearing one another, and forgiving one another."
- Colossians 3:12-13

SELF CONTROL – She encouraged David not to get back at Nabal but to go away in peace.
"Do not avenge yourselves [get even], for it is written, 'Vengeance is Mine, I will repay,' says the Lord."
- Romans 12:19

DIAMANTE

A diamante is a form of poetry that has 7 lines. It has the shape of a diamond because the 1st and 7th lines have one word (nouns), the 2nd and 6th lines have 2 words (adjectives/descriptions), the 3rd and 5th lines have 3 words (ending in ing), and the 4th line has 4 words (nouns).

The first 3½ lines of the poem are about a person, place or thing. The next 3½ lines of the poem are about an opposite person, place or thing such as summer and winter or day and night. Here are two examples about Abigail and Nabal.

Which fruit of the Spirit words can you find in Abigail's sections?

Abigail
Kind Faithful
Loving Praising Giving
Peacemaker Wife **Husband Sheepmaster**
Working Feasting Dying
Wealthy Selfish
Nabal

Nabal
Rich Mean
Hating Unfeeling Appalling
Farmer Boss **Homemaker Diplomat**
Sharing Serving Charming
Gentle Patient
Abigail

GRANDPARENTS AND GREAT-GRANDPARENTS

Do you know your mom's or dad's grandmother or grandfather? They would be your great-grandparents and are probably more than 70 years old. If you have parents, grandparents, and great-grandparents in your life, you are blessed. I have a very special picture from when I was about 3 years old. It includes me, my sisters, one brother, and some of our cousins with my Grandma Susie and her mother, Great-grandma Knee, who was very old.

It is important to be very careful around older people especially so they do not fall. You should also treat them with great respect in your actions and how you talk to them. You might have to speak up a little so they can hear you. But they can tell you many wonderful stories of when they were children and how different life was back then. They didn't have computers, cell phones, or microwaves when they were children.

Some people like to trace their history back for hundreds of years to find out who their great-great-great-great-great-grandparents were and where they lived. This is called a genealogy.

There are several places in the Bible where we can read genealogies, but they mostly include just the men's names. It's kind of boring for us to read, but it was important for their family history. King Asa in the Old Testament had a grandmother named Maachah, but she did not love and serve God (1 Kings 15:13). We know Timothy's godly grandmother was Lois (2 Timothy 1:5). We don't know much about great-grandmothers of the Bible without studying the history of Israel. But we do know about King David's wonderful great-grandparents, Boaz and Ruth.

If you have grandparents and great-grandparents, take time to get to know them and enjoy special times together.

DAVID'S FAMILY

As the youngest son, David ended up being the one to take care of the family's sheep. His family lived in Bethlehem. That is important to remember for later. While he was watching the sheep, David praised God. He wrote many of the Psalms in the Bible. You might already know Psalm 23 where he writes about God being like a shepherd and us being His sheep.

We've learned about David after he was a shepherd. He was a soldier for a while before he became King. And we learned about his wife Abigail. But David had another important and godly lady in his family. She was his great-grandmother, Ruth. We don't know if she was still living when David was born. You must remember he was the youngest of 8 boys in his family, and his grandparents and great-grandparents would have been old if they were still living.

David's father, Jesse, owned many sheep. While David was still a shepherd, before he killed Goliath, the Bible says that Jesse was already old (1 Samuel 17:12). He lived in Bethlehem. Do you suppose that David took care of Jesse's sheep in the same field where the shepherds saw the angels many years later when Jesus was born?

Jesse's father (David's grandfather) was Obed. About the only thing the Bible tells about Obed is who his father was and who his son was. He probably lived in Bethlehem.

Obed's father (David's great-grandfather) was Boaz. He was a very kind man who had fields and many servants. Boaz married Ruth. They lived in Bethlehem.

DAVID'S GREAT-GRANDMOTHER RUTH

The story of Ruth is in a small book of the Bible named Ruth. Ruth was not born in Israel. A family from the town of Bethlehem in Israel came to live in her country. The family had a dad, a mom, and two boys. One brother fell in love with Ruth and married her. The other brother got married, too. Then the dad and both brothers died. The mom (Naomi) and the two young wives were very sad. When the mom decided to move back to Bethlehem, Ruth insisted on going with her. She packed and traveled along because she loved Naomi and wanted to live in Israel and worship God.

When they got back to Bethlehem, Ruth told Naomi that she would gather (glean) the wheat and barley that was left in the fields. God directed Ruth to the field of Boaz, a kind, rich man. He noticed Ruth (maybe because she was pretty and a hard worker) and asked who she was. When he found out that she left her family and country to come and take care of Naomi, Boaz came over to Ruth and blessed her and told her not to go to another field. He even told his workers to leave extra wheat and barley for her to pick up.

When harvest time was finished, Boaz and Ruth got married! Then Ruth had a baby. The ladies in Bethlehem were so happy—mostly for Naomi to be a grandmother. What a special story for God to share with us.

God has a special story for your life, too. Make sure the Fruit of the Spirit is growing in your life as you wait to see how God will use you.

RUTH'S FRUIT

As we study Ruth, we find out that she also had a good heart and showed the Fruit of the Spirit to those around her.

LOVE – Ruth loved her first husband's mother, Naomi. She loved her so much that she was willing to leave her own country and relatives when Naomi decided to move back to Bethlehem. Ruth went along to take care of Naomi. By the end of the story, Ruth also fell in love with Boaz and got married!

JOY – Ruth experienced much sorrow and sadness in her young life, but once she knew God, she had a new joy. Of course, getting married to Boaz and having a son gave her much joy, also.

PEACE – During times of not knowing how things would work out, Ruth had peace knowing God's will for her was best. He had it all planned.

PATIENCE – The customs in Israel in those days are strange to us. Naomi told Ruth to go to Boaz and tell him that he was their close relative and it was his duty to marry Ruth.

She did that—then she waited patiently to see what would happen. And he did marry her.

KINDNESS – Ruth was very useful and kind to Naomi by providing food for her and making sure she was taken care of. She spoke gently and sweetly to her.

GOODNESS – The Bible does not say anything bad about Ruth. She displayed God's goodness to all those around her.

FAITHFULNESS – Ruth stayed with Naomi and went out to the fields day after day to get the food they needed to live. She was a hard worker. God promises to be faithful to us when we love and serve Him.

GENTLENESS – When Boaz saw Ruth working in his field, he asked who she was and found out about her taking care of Naomi. Boaz came over and talked to Ruth. The Bible tells us that she bowed to the ground and asked, "Why have I found favor in your eyes, that you should take notice of me?"

SELF CONTROL – Ruth could have been upset because of bad things that seemed to happen in her life. She could have gone looking for another husband. But she had self control as she waited for God to work His plans.

TWO DIAMANTES ABOUT RUTH AND BOAZ

Widow
Sad Poor
Wondering Thinking Doubting
Worker Traveler **Believer Friend**
Loving Caring Giving
Wealthy Happy
Wife

Boaz
Kind Fair
Working Protecting Loving
Husband Father **Wife Mother**
Giving Believing Serving
Brave Loyal
Ruth

KING DAVID'S GREAT- GREAT- GREAT- . . . GRANDDAUGHTER

One thousand years is a LONG time. No one lives that long. About 1,000 years after King David, Abigail, and Ruth lived, people still lived in Bethlehem, including shepherds. Some families had moved to other towns. A young girl who was David's great-great-great-. . . granddaughter, Mary, lived in another town. She was getting ready to marry David's great-great-great-. . . grandson, Joseph. She must have been very happy. One day she was very surprised when an angel appeared and told her that she would be the mother of God's Son, Jesus.

Mary, also, showed the Fruit of the Spirit in her life. She was gentle and humble when she learned this. She didn't get proud and think she was better than all the other young ladies. She was joyful. You can read in Luke 1:46-55 how she praised God that He would choose her to be Jesus' mother. You can be sure God's choice for the mother of Jesus would be a godly young lady who had the Fruit of the Spirit

When it was almost time for Jesus to be born, every family had to go to their family's town to be registered for taxes. Mary and Joseph had to go to Bethlehem because that's where their family came from. They made the trip, and you know the story about what happened in the stable in Bethlehem when Jesus was born and how the shepherds out in the fields where David had been a shepherd 1,000 years earlier came to see Jesus.

It is exciting to see how God used Ruth, Abigail, and Mary in David's family to work out God's plan for a Savior to be born who would die for our sins.

ABIGAIL'S ORCHARD PUZZLE

```
B L P R V Q X P S N E O Y P J
S E I S U B Y Q S W Y V E O L
K S T A U T R Y E F M A O X J
S I E H G K H K N D C F J L B
I E N N L I E A D E W G E R S
C I L D E E B B O B V V S T P
I Z N F N L H A O L J X U A I
K I N G C E T E G J T F S K R
P W K Y I O S N M U I A M P I
W K M D Q C N S E O U I A M T
Z B U S T R M T F G R T R V Z
E C N E I T A P R F F H Y N R
D A V I D M U M S O R F N S H
K L D R N I X M F K L U O B Y
R K Q F J E A D O X F L Q E B
```

ABIGAIL
FAITHFUL
GOODNESS
KINDNESS
MARY
RUTH
BETHLEHEM
FRUIT
JESUS
KING
PATIENCE
SELF CONTROL
DAVID
GENTLENESS
JOY
LOVE
PEACE
SPIRIT

9. Orf twih odG goinnth liwl eb slimesipob.

10. Het roLd si ym phredesh; I halls ton tawn.

11. Lendrich, yobe oury narpets ni het rold, rof tish si ghrit.

12. Eb dink ot noe thranoe, derentedearth, gingiforv noe the-noar.

13. Tel verey nam eb fwits ot reah, wols ot pakes, owls ot whart.

14. Ot mih how skown ot od dogo dan soed ton od ti, ot mih ti si ins.

15. Tub het trifu fo het siptir si voel, oyj, aceep, grinsurffer-glon, sendskin, sendsogo, faintshelfus, glessenten, fels-loctron. Stainag cush reeth si on wal.

(Rom. 3:23)   (Acts 16:31)   (John 8:32)   (Rom. 6:23)

(Eph. 2:8)   (Matt. 6:21)   (Luke 19:10)   (John 3:3)

(Luke 1:37)   (Psa. 23:1)   (Eph. 6:1)   (Eph. 4:32)

(James 1:19)   (James 4:17)   (Eph. 5:22-23)

26   **FUN WITH WORDS**

SCRAMBLED BIBLE VERSES

(References at the end if you need help.)

1. Lal evah nisden dan moce roths fo het yorgl fo dGo.

2. Vielebe no het dorL seJus thirCs dan oyu lashl eb vased.

3. Ouy halls nowk het hurtt dan het hurtt halls tes ouy reef.

4. Het gasew fo ins si ethad, tub het tgif fo dGo si treelan file.

5. Rof yb cager ear ouy vased hrougtg hatif, dan tath ton fo vesselrouy ti si het tgif fo dGo.

6. Rof hewer uoyr seaurret si reeht ruoy earth lilw eb laso.

7. Rof het ons fo nam si moce ot ekse dan ot vase hatt hichw saw stol.

8. Sunsel eon si robn ginaa, eh noncat ese het minkdog fo oGd.

FUN WITH BRADY
WORD SEARCH

```
T F D U X F W B M C G P U H O
N R E B O X R I K P R M F Z M
E I V H C O N Y L O P O N O M
D E A M T E S S V H L U X C I
U N S H C P E W S R E B M U N
T D E R N N K I J S Q D S X C
S R A W H C A N W R Z T C V I
E F O G E L C G J O E H A G W
T V S E A I N M Q N E M I R N
Y U I M H Y A Q A C B M Y F T
N R N T D C P L K F L R A Z U
O O R G A X P E Z E C Y A T S
S U A O B E R B B V D L G D H
B Z K W S S R A Y F V L G A Y
K Y E F G G Y C C O U S I N A
```

ART
BRADY
BROTHER
CHECKERS
COUSIN
CREATIVE
FRIEND

LEGO
MATH
MINECRAFT
MONOPOLY
NUMBERS
PANCAKES
PLANETS

SAVED
SON
SORRY
STUDENT
SWING

100% WORDS

When you have a page of math or other schoolwork to do, your teacher (or parents) will check over it to see if you did it correctly. If you wrote a wrong answer, they might put a check mark next to that. If you do everything correctly, perhaps they will put an A+ or a 100% at the top of your paper. That means you got ALL of them right—you didn't miss any of the problems.

ALL includes everything, everyone, everywhere, and always—without any exceptions. If you ate all the peanuts, no one else had any of them. If you walked all the way to the store, you didn't get a ride in a car or ride a bike part of the way. If you spent all of your money, there was not even one penny left over.

Romans 3:23 says "All have sinned." That means every single person who has ever lived on earth, except the Lord Jesus Christ, is a sinner who needs to accept His free gift of salvation in order to become His child and spend eternity in heaven.

The suffix "omni" means all. Three words that use this suffix refer to God. *Omnipotent* means all powerful. Revelation 19:6 tells us that "The Lord, God omnipotent reigns."

Omniscient means all knowing. I John 3:20 says, "God is greater than our heart, and knows all things." *Omnipresent* means all present—everywhere at the same time. Psalm 139:7-12 reminds us that wherever we go—God is with us.

Even though you cannot see God, it's important to remember that He is with you, He knows you, and He has power to help you when you need His strength to do right. Trust Him!

Genesis 1:16 includes the idea of these three words. On the 4th day of creation, God made **two** great lights **to** shine in the sky. What shines during the day? Which one shines at night? Then it says, "He made the stars also" (**too**).

1 Kings 12:28: "Therefore the king asked advice, made **two** calves of gold, and said **to** the people, "It is **too** much for you **to** go up **to** Jerusalem."

TOO MANY TWOS TO COUNT

You need to know about another set of homonyms. The first one is spelled **TO**. We use it often to explain things like what we are going to do, where we are going to do it, or how we are going to do it. "I am making a cake to take to the party."

To is also used to tell the score of a ballgame: "We are winning, 7 to 4!"

The next word begins the same but adds another o on the end: **TOO**. This isn't used as often as TO. Sometimes it is used the same as "also" would be used. Other times it is used to show an amount or size such as too much, too large, too short, or too full.

"I like pizza, and I like ice cream, too."

"My pants are too tight because I ate too much pizza and ice cream."

The third word has a strange spelling but is pronounced the same as to and too. It is the number **TWO** (2). "I know a little boy who just turned two years old."

Can you fill in the correct words
in the following sentence?

I have _____ many clothes _____ fit into my _____ suitcases.

remember. It would be used in a sentence like this: "They're almost finished raking the leaves."

See if you can make up some sentences using all three of these words. Here's one to get you started: They're going over there to see their friends.

20   FUN WITH WORDS

THERE, THEIR, AND THEY'RE

The English language has words that sound alike but are spelled differently and mean different things. These are called homonyms. Here are several ways to help you remember how to use the <u>right</u> words when you <u>write</u> them.

"The" is an easy word that we use dozens of times a day. Three words that begin with those same letters cause confusion for many people. They are <u>there</u>, <u>their</u>, and <u>they're</u>. They all sound the same, but they mean something different.

THERE can mean a place, such as: "My house is over there." It is also used to begin a sentence, such as: "There are enough pieces of candy for everyone."

If you take away the first letter, you have the word <u>here</u>. This word is used to mean the time or place where you are now, such as: "There are enough pieces of candy for everyone who is here."

THEIR also begins with the word <u>the</u>. It sounds like <u>there</u>, but it is used when you are talking about something that belongs to someone else, such as: "Their mother had a beautiful baby girl yesterday."

THEY'RE is a contraction. It's a shortened form of <u>they</u> <u>are</u>. The <u>a</u> is missing, so an apostrophe is put in place of the <u>a</u> and the space between the words. This one should be easy to

SILENT AND LISTEN

It's hard to be quiet—especially if you are with a friend. You always have things to talk about with your friends. But there are times that you must be quiet. In school and Sunday school class, you need to be quiet while your teacher teaches the lesson and gives instructions. The library is a place where people expect you to be quiet so they can read and study. There are plenty of places where you can talk and make noise—like at recess or at the park.

Silent is another word for quiet. Think about the Christmas Carol, "Silent Night." It was probably pretty quiet late that night when the shepherds went away, the animals went to sleep, and Jesus was laid in the manger.

If you rearrange the letters in SILENT, you can make another word of something you should do when your parents or teachers are talking to you. Can you figure out what that word is? It begins with L_ _ _ _ _.

Sometimes your parents or teachers may say, "Be quiet and go to sleep," or "Be quiet and study." Learn how to be silent and listen. Be quiet and hear the birds. Be quiet and listen to what people are saying to you.

"Let every man be swift to hear, slow to speak" (James 1:19).

DANGER AND ANGER

Can you find the one letter that is different in the words danger and anger? ____ That was easy. Always remember that it is dangerous to be angry with others. Anger often causes us to do and say things that we shouldn't.

When Moses and the Israelites came out of Egypt, God called Moses to the top of the mountain and gave him the Ten Commandments. When Moses came down from the mountain, the people were worshipping a golden idol. Moses was angry about their sin and threw down the tablet of commandments—breaking them (Exodus 32:1-19).

Later as they wandered through the wilderness for 40 years, God provided food and drink for them through miracles. One time He told Moses to *speak* to a rock and water would come out. Moses was so angry with the complaining people that he *hit* the rock with his staff. God had water come out, but He was sad that Moses disobeyed him. Because of that, Moses was not permitted to go into the promised land (Numbers 20:1-12).

God is angry about sin. One day when Jesus lived on the earth, He went into the temple and found people buying and selling things there instead of worshipping God. He got angry and turned over the tables and told the people to take their things and money out of the house of prayer (Luke 20:45-46).

Angry people might do very foolish things (Proverbs 14:17). People who are always angry should not be the ones you choose to have as friends (Proverbs 22:24). Remember: Add a D to anger, and you could be in danger.

ANGLE AND ANGEL

Look at these two words. They have the same letters—but the last two are reversed. One has a hard G sound; the other has a soft G sound.

The hard G sound is in the word angle. An angle is formed when two lines come together from different directions. The difference in the space determines the degree of the angle. Triangle and rectangle have the word angle in them. A triangle has 3 angles—one at each point. Squares and rectangles have 4 angles. The number 7 is an example of an angle.

An angel is one of God's helpers. Hebrews 1:14 says angels are sent by God to help those who believe in God for salvation. Maybe you can remember angel ends with gel—like what some people put on their hair. You can pretend that angels use gel to keep their wings stiff!

Many times in the Bible, angels were sent to help people or to give them a message from God. Angels came to Gideon, Daniel, Elisha, Peter, the women at Jesus' tomb, and others. However, my favorite angel story is in Luke 1 when the angel Gabriel came to tell Mary that she was going to be the mother of Baby Jesus. Then in Matthew 1 the angel came to Joseph to tell him the same thing. After Mary and Joseph traveled to Bethlehem and Jesus was born, the angels appeared to the shepherds to tell them. (Luke 2) That was a very special time.

What is your favorite "angel" story?

DEITY AND DIET

One of these words follows the I before E rule, the other does not follow the rule. It is important to know the difference. They look similar, they are pronounced differently; and their meanings are very different—not opposites, but different.

The word that follows the rule is <u>diet</u> with a long I sound followed by a short E sound. This word refers to our food. Most often when we hear or use that word it is in connection with trying to lose weight, but it's also used when talking about a healthy diet or a poor diet or a special diet because of food allergies. It's nice to have treats and snacks once in a while, but it is important for growing boys and girls to have a healthy diet so that their bones, teeth, and body grow strong.

<u>Deity</u> does not follow the rule. It has a long E sound followed by a short I sound. This is another word for God. Most versions of our Bible do not use this exact word, but the whole Bible is about the deity of God the Father, God the Son (Jesus), and God the Holy Spirit. He is the one and only true God. He is the only living God. (Hebrews 3:12) Many people worship idols or religious leaders who have already died. They can't help anyone. But God will never die and wants the whole world to know Him.

Make sure you eat a healthy diet—and that you worship the only one true Deity.

THE FIERY FURNACE

Some of you live near a fire station and hear sirens all times of the night and day. It's a sign that someone has a problem—a fire or an accident. When you hear a fire siren, it's a good idea to stop and pray that God will take care of the people.

The word fiery has a very tricky spelling because it comes from the word FIRE, but when you add the Y to the end, the E moves between the I and R. So it goes along with the I before E rule.

Of course, this makes me think about the fiery furnace in Daniel 3 when Nebuchadnezzar made a gold image and commanded people to bow down to it. When the horn sounded, everyone bowed down except for three Jewish fellows: Shadrach, Meshach, and Abed-Nego. The king gave them a second chance, but they still didn't do it. Because they refused to bow to anyone other than God, they were cast into the fiery furnace that was made 7 times hotter than before. God took care of them so that they were not burned at all. The king let them out of the furnace, he glorified God, and even gave those three brave men better jobs.

Sadly many Christians, mostly in other countries, have been treated badly and suffered many things because of their belief in God. Some have been imprisoned and even killed. They knew that Jesus died for them, and they were not ashamed to die for Him.

Be brave and always do right. Jesus will be with you to help you to have the courage.

A FRIEND IS A FRIEND TO THE END

The word friend follows the "I before E" rule. Another way to remember it is that the word **end** is at the **end** of fri**end**: "A fri**end** is a fri**end** to the **end**." It is important to have good friends, and it is important to be a good friend.

David and Jonathan in the Bible were best friends. David's life was in danger because King Saul was jealous of David and threw a javelin at him several times. Jonathan, the prince, helped David escape danger (1 Samuel 20). Before they parted, they made a promise to each other that if one of them died, the other one would take care of his family. Jonathan died first in battle, and when David became King, he took care of Jonathan's crippled son, Mephibosheth, just like he took care of his own sons (2 Samuel 9).

Proverbs 18:24 tells about a Friend Who sticks closer to us than a brother—and that is Jesus. He should be your Best Friend Forever (BFF), because He loves you more than any of your other friends do. He loves you so much that He died on the cross to take away your sins. Have you asked Him to take them away? Hebrews 13:5 reminds us that Jesus will never leave us or turn against us—no matter what.

Make sure Jesus is your BFF and tell your other friends about Him. That's the best thing you can do for your friends.

DON'T BELIEVE A LIE

Believe and receive are two words that you will use many times in your life, so learn how to spell them now. Believe has the word lie in the middle. Don't believe a lie. Jesus used the words believe and receive many times because He wants you to believe that He loves you and died on the cross to take away your sins. That is His free gift to you. Now He wants you to receive that free gift called salvation so that you will be ready to live with Him forever in heaven.

DECEIVE

The word deceive means to trick someone and make them believe something that is not true. Satan is called the Deceiver. He tries to get people to believe the lie that we can be good enough to go to heaven without asking Jesus to take away our sins. He gets people to think if they give enough money to their church or if they just get baptized they will go to heaven.

Don't believe the deceiver's lie. Believe God and receive His gift today.

TRICKY WORD TRICKS

Our language has many rules for spelling words. It also contains words that sound alike but are spelled differently and have different meanings (homonyms); others are pronounced the same, they have different meanings, but the spelling may be the same or different (homophones). Synonyms are words that mean nearly the same thing but they are not spelled or pronounced the same. Opposite words are called antonyms. Because of so many words from which to choose, things can get a little confusing sometimes. That's why it's nice to have some tricks to help remember the difference.

I BEFORE E

Many times teachers give little tricks or hints to help you remember things. One trick that almost everyone learns is: "I before E except after C." This means that when a word has I and E together, sometimes the I comes before the E—like in the words *believe* and *friend*. But most of the time when they come after C, the E comes before the I—like in the words *receive* and *deceive*. Many words in our language don't follow that rule, but quite a few of them do.

OUT OF SIGHT, OUT OF _____

When babies are learning to hold onto toys, they often drop them on the floor. The baby doesn't know where the toy went, so he just looks at something else. If he doesn't see it, he forgets about it. That's what we call "out of sight, out of mind." When we see things, we think about them. As we grow up we figure out that we can think about things even if we can't see them. But it's hard to remember everything we should, so we make notes to remind ourselves—especially as we get older.

Since Jesus went back to heaven 2,000 years ago, nobody on Earth has seen Him. We learn about Him from the Bible. We are reminded of Him as we look around and see His beautiful creation. We can think of God and pray to Him anytime, but because we can't see Him, many times we don't think about Him until something bad happens and we suddenly think to ask Him for help.

We are never out of God's sight. He knows everything about us—even how many hairs we have (Luke 12:7). God never even sleeps. He always sees us, so He never forgets about us. Our Lord's eyes move back and forth across the earth, to show himself strong (2 Chronicles 16:9).

So, don't forget about your family, friends and missionaries when you are not with them. And for sure, don't forget about what Jesus did for you.

THE GRASS IS ALWAYS _____

Pop and I enjoy walking around our neighborhood looking at the pretty flowers and nice houses. Some lawns have dandelions and bare spots, while other lawns have been treated with chemicals to kill the weeds and fertilizer to make the grass grow better. Of course, some other lawns don't look so good. Often we look at what other people have and think we would be happy if we had that. But things aren't always as good up close as they look from a distance.

Abraham and his nephew Lot had herds and flocks of animals. They also had herdsmen to help take care of the many animals. They traveled around so they would have fresh grass for their animals. Sometimes their herdsmen got angry with each other—trying to make sure their animals got the best grazing area. Abraham didn't like this, so he told Lot to choose which direction he wanted for his animals, and then Abraham would take his animals the other direction. Lot slowly turned around, looking in all directions. He chose the area that was well watered and had the best green grass. Perhaps he thought he would be happy; however, his green fields were near two cities full of wicked people. God destroyed those cities with fire. Only Lot and two of his daughters escaped.

Perhaps Abraham's grass wasn't quite as green as Lot's, but Abraham, his servants, and his animals were safe and content (Genesis 13 & 19).

Just because something looks better, doesn't mean it actually is. Check out all the facts before you decide which choice is best. Then be content.

SEEING IS _____

Sometimes we hear things that just seem impossible. Soldiers come home from the war and surprise their children at school. The children wouldn't believe their Dad was there unless they saw him. It's hard to believe without seeing, but men have walked on a rope across Niagara Falls. People have come away from terrible accidents or tornados without any cuts or broken bones. My aunt went to the hospital to have a baby and found out she had twins. Boy, was she surprised! She had to see both of them to believe it.

Bible words for believing are trust and faith. Faith believes even when it can't understand how something could be possible. One of Jesus' disciples was not with the others when Jesus appeared to them following His death and resurrection. Doubting Thomas said that unless he could see Jesus' hands and put his fingers into the nail prints and put his hand into Jesus' side where the spear pierced Him, he would not believe. Eight days later Thomas was with the rest of the disciples when Jesus appeared; then he believed. Jesus said, "Blessed are those who have not seen and yet have believed" (John 20:24-29).

Even though we were not there when Jesus died and rose again, by faith we believe that He did that for us. Someday we will see Him. Believe—you'll see.

THE BEST THINGS IN LIFE ARE _____

Pop and I just came from town with a free Frosty from Wendy's and a free frappé from McDonald's. We had coupons and didn't have to pay anything for those treats. This morning we had a "free" breakfast because someone gave us a gift card to a restaurant. Sometimes after people have yard sales, they will put the unsold items at the end of their driveway with a "Free" sign. It's fun to get free stuff. These things are free to us, but it cost someone else to give these gifts to us.

Think about the free things God gives to us: sunshine, the air we breathe, snow, rain, the beautiful sunrise and sunset to enjoy. We can hear the birds singing and watch the butterflies for free. These are truly gifts—things we get to enjoy without working or paying for them.

Of course, the best gift of all is something else from God. "The gift of God is eternal life in Christ Jesus our Lord" (Romans 6:23). The gift of salvation is something that we cannot work for. We cannot earn it. We cannot pay for it. It is something God wants us to have just because He loves us and wants us to be in heaven with Him. All we have to do is realize we are a sinner and ask God to save us from our sins. This is a free gift to us, but it did cost Jesus His life because He died on the cross to take the punishment in our place.

Enjoy all of God's free gifts, but make sure you accept His gift of salvation. And share the Good News with others.

BE A GOOD _____

When your parents take you to class at school or church, do they say, "Now, be a good boy"? When you have a babysitter and your parents are going out the door, what do they say? "Be good." If you are going to spend the night at your friend's house, they probably tell you they love you, hope you have a good time, and to be good!

What do your parents mean when they tell you to be good? Usually they mean don't be bad. It's not always easy to be good, but with God's help we can usually be pretty good.

However, the Bible tells us to go beyond **being** good—we are to **do** good things for others. Ephesians 2:10 reminds us that God created us to do good works. That is our job while we are here on earth. You probably know the Golden Rule: "Do unto others as you would have them do unto you." You want people to be kind and helpful to you. So that's how you should be to them. It's easy to be kind to people who are kind to us. But the Bible says we are to do good to all men (Galatians 6:10). Jesus said, "Love your enemies, do good to those who hate you" (Luke 6:27). Now that's a tough assignment for adults, let alone children.

The next time someone is mean to you, think of something kind you can do for them like smiling, sharing some cookies, choosing them to be on your team, helping them with homework, picking up trash, or raking grass.

Can you do it? YES YOU CAN!

DO WHAT I SAY, NOT WHAT I _____

As you get older, you will recognize people who tell you what you should or should not do, but they don't follow the same advice or rules. For instance, a doctor may tell people to eat properly and get enough exercise—but the doctor weighs 400 pounds! A teacher might tell you not to smoke because it causes lung cancer, but when that teacher is alone, he smokes. Some preachers who tell people to read the Bible and pray every day don't read their Bible or pray every day. A dad might tell his children to eat their vegetables, but guess what—he doesn't eat vegetables! Perhaps a mom tells her children to obey the speed limit, but she gets stopped by the police for speeding. You can probably think of many more examples.

People who do the opposite of what they tell others to do are called hypocrites. They are fakes. They act and sound like one kind of person, but they really are a different kind of person. Jesus had many things to say to and about hypocrites when He lived on the earth. He described them as people who say the right things to Him and about Him, but in their hearts they don't really mean it (Matthew 15:8). They are proud and want people to think they are really good, but it's just for show. Matthew 23:2-3 says that the scribes and Pharisees were like that. They put heavy burdens on men's shoulders, but they wouldn't lift a finger to help.

Think about what you are saying today—does it match what's in your heart? Be a true follower of Jesus. Oh and eat your peas, too!

THAT'S NOT _____

How many times have you said, "That's not fair"? Perhaps your brother or sister got a larger piece of cake or they got to go somewhere and you had to stay home or they got to stay up later than you. Of course, if you were the one with the larger piece of cake or got to go somewhere or stay up later, you probably wouldn't say, "That's not fair." You'd feel pretty special—perhaps a bit proud. Things happen every day that don't seem fair. But that's the way life is.

Getting to go to heaven isn't fair. Because of our sinful hearts, none of us deserve to go to heaven. But God loved us so much that He made a special plan that Jesus would come down to earth as a baby, grow up, and die on the cross to pay the punishment for our sins. Was that fair—for Jesus to be punished for our sins? Of course not! But He did it because He loved us. Can you say John 3:16 with me? "For God so loved the world that He gave His only begotten Son, that whoever believes in Him should not perish but have everlasting life."

When we get something good that we don't deserve, it's called grace. Be thankful when you receive grace, but don't grumble and complain when someone else receives it. Romans 12:15 tells us to be happy (rejoice) with others who are happy. It's not easy, especially at first, but give it a try.

4   **FUN WITH WORDS**

LIKE FATHER, LIKE _____

Many times people will look at a boy and say, "I can tell whose son he is. He looks just like his daddy." or "He has his daddy's eyes, but his nose looks like his mommy's." Other times it's not so much how a child looks, but rather the way he talks and does things. Boys want to be just like Dad; girls want to be like Mom. Perhaps they like a certain sports team because that's Dad's favorite team. Some boys want to grow up and do the kind of job their dad does. That's why we say, "Like father, like son." Children imitate what their parents do and say.

When Jesus was a boy, He learned to do the things Joseph did—they were carpenters. The furniture they made must have been the best furniture in Galilee. People spoke about Jesus being the carpenter (Mark 6:3) and the son of the carpenter (Matthew 13:55).

When Jesus was 12 years old, Mary and Joseph took Him on a trip to Jerusalem for the Passover. After the feast, Mary and Joseph started home with many other people. At the end of the day, they could not find Jesus. They walked back to Jerusalem and found Him in the temple talking to the teachers. Mary scolded Jesus because they spent so much time looking for Him. Jesus said, "Did you not know that I must be about My Father's business?" (Luke 2:49). You see, Jesus really was and is the Son of God. He was being just like His Father—God.

When we become Christians, God is our heavenly Father. We are to be like Him as much as we can. You can do this by learning His Word.

IT'S ALL ABOUT _____

"Give it to me. I had it first. I want that. That's mine! I deserve it. His piece is bigger than mine. That's **not** what I wanted."

This world is full of selfish people. Most people want things for themselves. They think "It's all about ME" and the world should revolve around them. They want to have the best bicycle, the biggest collection of LEGOS, the newest clothing, the biggest piece of cake, or the prettiest doll. They think they should win every game and contest. They are so selfish, they don't think about other people.

A bumper sticker said, "It's all about my dog." A dog? Your pet should not be the most important thing in your life. You should take care of your pet and enjoy it, but it should not be more important than loving God and other people. Did you notice that the word "dog" has the same letters as "God"—just in a different order? We should say, "It's all about my God." He made us, Jesus died on the cross for us, and He gives us what we need. It's all about Him! We cannot do anything without Him. Psalm 100:3 says, "Know that the Lord, He is God; It is He who has made us." We are nothing without Him.

The Bible says if we make anything more important than God, that thing becomes an idol. We worship that thing rather than worshiping and loving God with all our heart. Make sure God is more important than yourself and what you want.

2   FUN WITH WORDS

WRITING ON THE _____

Do you know that some young children write or draw on the walls in their house? Maybe they forget that markers or crayons are to be used on paper. One special 4-year-old boy was able to write his name, so he wrote on the wall that he loved his Pop (because he could spell Pop, too). Pop was glad that the boy expressed his love for him, but he wasn't glad that it was on the wall. It takes a lot of scrubbing to get crayon or marker off the wall. Sometimes, the wall has to be painted to cover it.

Someone wrote on the wall in the Bible. The message was true but it wasn't happy. You know about how Daniel and his friends were taken from their country to Babylon by Nebuchadnezzar, who also took the gold and silver items from the temple. Later, Nebuchadnezzar's son was the king. One night the king gave a party and used the gold and silver things from God's temple. All of a sudden, a hand appeared and began writing on the wall. It was the hand of God writing a message in a language the king could not understand. He became frightened and needed someone to read the message. Daniel told him it was a message from God. An army from another country was coming and another king would be in charge. And that's exactly what happened—that night.

It's great to express your love for people—but just remember to do it on paper, not on the wall.

FILL IN THE BLANK

Teachers use tests to find out if students have learned what was taught. Spelling tests are easier to study for because the students know the words they will have to write. Essay tests are harder for many students because they are expected to write many sentences about a subject. Multiple choice tests at least give the right answer. Students choose which answer they think is correct. True/False tests can be tricky, but students have a 50/50 chance at getting it right. Another kind of test is fill in the blank. Some teachers in Christian schools use fill in the blank for Bible verse tests like this:

For _____ so _____ the world

God _____ us and sent his _____

All have _____

_____ on the _____ Jesus _____

The following pages include some fill in the blank statements that you may have heard before.

ai

TABLE OF CONTENTS
FUN WITH WORDS

Fill In The Blank 1
    Writing on the _____ 2
    It's All About _____ 3
    Like Father, Like _____ 4
    That's Not _____ 5
    Do What I Say, Not What I _____ 6
    Be a Good _____ 7
    The Best Things in Life Are _____ 8
    Seeing is _____ 9
    The Grass Is Always _____ 10
    Out of Sight, Out of _____ 11

Tricky Word Tricks 12
    I Before E 12
    Don't Believe a Lie 13
    Deceive 13
    A Friend to the End 14
    Fiery Furnace 15
    Deity and Diet 16
    Angle and Angel 17
    Danger and Anger 18
    Silent and Listen 19
    There, Their, and They're 20
    Too Many Twos to Count 22
    100% Words 24

Fun with Brady Word Search 25
Scrambled Bible Verses 26

iii

dedicated to
BRADY DOUGLAS WILLIAMS

FUN WITH WORDS

BY ELAINE WILLIAMS

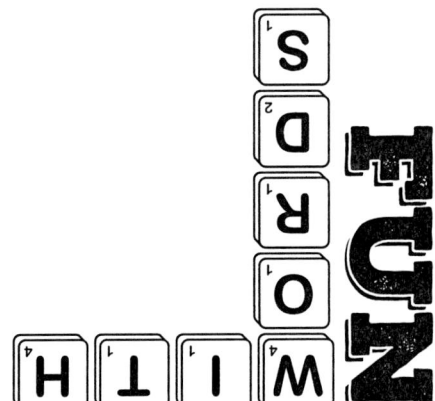